Nichola Fletcher has written nearly a dozen highly acclaimed books about food, including *Charlemagne's Tablecloth, Nichola Fletcher's Ultimate Venison Cookery, Caviar: A Global History* and Birlinn's *The Venison Bible*, all of which have won major awards. In 2014 she was given an MBE for services to the venison industry.

The
Scottish Oats
Bible

Nichola Fletcher

Illustrated by Bob Dewar

BIRLINN

To Martha,
who is the real baker in our family

First published in 2016 by
Birlinn Limited
West Newington House
10 Newington Road
Edinburgh
EH9 1QS

www.birlinn.co.uk

ISBN: 978 1 78027 364 8

British Library Cataloguing-in-Publication Data
A catalogue record for this book is available
from the British Library

Designed and typeset by Mark Blackadder

Printed and bound by Bell & Bain Ltd, Glasgow

Contents

Soup and savoury dishes

Desserts

Baking

Acknowledgments

My thanks to all those in the oatmeal trade who have patiently answered my questions. And my thanks to the following authors whose writings have inspired me: Meg Dods, F. Marian McNeill, Alexander Fenton, Catherine Brown, Annette Hope and Sue Lawrence. Finally my thanks to all my tasters (especially John) who have munched and drunk their way through these recipes.

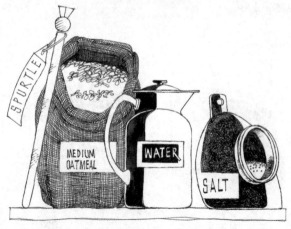

Introduction

A field of oats, with the delicate ears formed but not yet ripe and waving in a cool breeze, is a beautiful sight. A soft bluey green like a misty day promises good things to come when the grains will turn to a deep, rich gold. Oats thrive in our cool damp Scottish climate, which is why they form such a pivotal part of the traditional Scots diet. Although widely grown from early times, after the agricultural revolution in the seventeenth century, oats became the pre-eminent food grain in Scotland, supplanting beremeal.

Delve a little into the way in which oats were used and you realise just how important they were. As well as porridge and oatcakes – once the two backbones of our society – oatmeal was used for birth, baptism and wedding ceremonies, to encourage good harvests, to make bannocks at Beltane for charming spirits, as travellers' food, and even to form a vessel in which to cook fish livers. Oats were used to cleanse the skin and were fermented to make refreshing drinks and other historic foods which are ripe for revival. They made comforting cold-weather tonics, crisp biscuits, sweeties for children, and sustaining food and

Golspie Mill

drink that kept men and women working their long, hard hours. Oats were a sufficiently important part of a rural university student's diet to be acknowledged by a Meal Monday holiday in February, when students could return home for replenishments.

The names of oatmeal dishes are poetic and quaint: sowans and skirlie, hodgils and hatted kit, brose and bannock, crowdie mowdie and mealie candy, meal-and-ale and white caudle, fitless cock and caper, soor poos and drammach, blenshaw and stoorum. The list goes on. But they are all the product of the oatmeal sack.

Scottish oatmeal mills

At one time there were hundreds of meal mills dotted all over the country. Ian Miller, a former managing director of John Hogarth Ltd, remembers going to Pitlochry in 1956 for the oatmeal millers' annual gathering. It lasted for three days, and included tennis, golf and bowling. Even then there were still a hundred mills represented. Now these have dwindled to the five remaining mills listed – from north to south – below.

Golspie Mill is a picturesque water-powered mill built in 1862 on the Dunrobin side of Golspie. It was restored in 1992 and now produces oatmeal on a fairly small scale as well as beremeal, peasemeal, and wheat and rye flour.

Hamlyns Scottish Oats is at Boyndie, outside Banff, where a wind turbine powers their state-of-the-art factory. They still use millstones to grind their oatmeal though. They are an amalgamation of several farming businesses and cooperatives including Grampian Oats, and their brand goes back to 1965. Their retail packs are widely available. Hamlyns also supply meal for the famous Stockan's Orkney oatcakes and Stoats oat products, and they sponsor the World Porridge Championships.

Oatmeal of Alford has an attractive old stone watermill at Montgarrie, near Alford. The present mill dates from 1882 although it was built on the foundations of a much earlier watermill. The oats are dried on a perforated iron floor over a stone furnace. Their organic oats are grown at the family farm near Laurencekirk and are certified gluten-free.

Scotts Porage Oats (Quaker oats), near Cupar in Fife, must be the best-known brand of rolled oats – the distinctive shot-putting Highlander has been on their packs since 1924. The firm started in 1880 in Glasgow, then moved to Edinburgh and finally settled in Fife in 1947. It is the largest oat mill in western Europe.

John Hogarth Ltd's current Victorian building stands by the Tweed at Kelso on a site that has had a mill since before the Abbey was built in 1128. Since they are predominantly wholesalers and don't have their own retail brand, their name is not well known to the public, but they produce oatmeal and pearl barley for many well-known brands, currently including Nairn's Oatcakes and Aberfeldy Oatmeal.

Nutrition

Samuel Johnson's famous dictionary entry about oats ('A grain, which in England is generally given to horses, but in Scotland supports the people') has become a cliché. But when Johnson came to Scotland in 1773, Sir Walter Scott was sufficiently anxious about that snub to have written to his son-in-law: 'What meal does Johnnie want for his porridge? I will send it up from Abbotsford. I think it will agree with him better than the southern food of horses.' And during Johnson's visit, the economist and opinion-former Lord Elibank's excellent riposte was, 'Very true. And where else will you see such *men*, and such *horses*?' He didn't need a nutritionist to point out the advantages of a diet rich in oatmeal. He knew that oats are deeply satisfying, lift the spirit, stave off hunger pangs for long hours, and taste good forby.

Oats are mainly composed of carbohydrate that contains the soluble fibre beta-glucan which is good for digestion and which has been shown to lower LDL (bad) cholesterol. It also seems to help lower high blood pressure.

In addition, oats contain a protein called avenin, some fat and some calcium. They are a good source of folic acid and iron, of vitamin B1 and zinc, which helps people to absorb the iron. Being high in magnesium, they also help to reduce the risk of type 2 diabetes. As a source of vitamin B6, they help the central nervous system to function and also to carry oxygen around in the bloodstream.

Oats themsleves contain no gluten, which makes them unsuitable for springy-textured bread and pasta-making, but very useful for the increasing numbers of people with wheat intolerances. Gluten-free oats can be eaten by many coeliacs, but not all because the protein in oats (avenin) is similar to gluten and causes a reaction in some coeliacs.

Oat groats and oatmeal have a low Glycaemic Index (GI) and are excellent for slow-release carbohydrate energy. They also seem to help with anxiety and depression. Rolled oats and flour, however, have a medium or high GI and can produce sugar 'highs' and 'lows' like other processed carbohydrates, so are less good for sustaining the full-stomach feeling.

The different types of oats

Oat groats: the whole grain, including the bran, which has had the indigestible outer husk removed. Good for overnight porridge and risotto-like dishes. Most oat groats sold today are heat-stabilised to prevent them from going

rancid, which they can otherwise do very quickly. Low GI.
Oat bran: the fine skin covering oat groats. Highly nutritious, it reduces cholesterol as well as adding valuable soluble fibre to the diet. Pinhead and medium oatmeal both include the oat bran. It is useful for slimmers as it reduces the calorie intake and swells in the stomach. Low GI.

Pinhead oats: also called **steel cut oats or groats**, and (outside Scotland and Ireland), **Scots or Irish oats**. This is the whole groat that has been either ground by a millwheel or, more commonly nowadays, sliced with steel cutters into three or four pieces. **Coarse or rough oatmeal** is not much smaller than pinhead but, being milled, is more floury. Low GI.

Medium oatmeal: the most common oatmeal used in Scottish cooking and therefore often simply called '**oatmeal**', this is the groat that has been ground (mostly stoneground) into a meal whose largest grains are 1–2mm in diameter. It should not be confused with rolled oats below. Low GI.

Fine oatmeal: the groat which has been very finely ground until it resembles wheaten flour, and still includes the bran. However, the terms oat flour and fine oatmeal are often interchangeable so if the presence or absence of bran is important, check with your supplier. Fine oatmeal and oat flour are not always easy to buy but you can easily transform rolled oats into fine oatmeal by blitzing them in a food processor and sieving them. Medium GI.

Oat flour: fine oatmeal which has had the bran sifted out. It has no gluten so is unsuitable for bread making but is used in cakes, pastry, scones and for thickening sauces. Medium-high GI.

Jumbo oats: also called **old-fashioned oats**, these are oat groats, steamed for some minutes to partially cook them, and then rolled to make a large flake. They are good for adding texture to porridge, oatcakes, muesli and granola. Medium GI.

Rolled oats: also called **quick oats, flaked oats, or porridge oats**, these are made from pinhead oats, steamed to partially cook them, and then rolled to make a smaller flake that cooks quicker than jumbo oats. Medium GI.

Instant oats have been precooked for longer so they cook instantly. However, the loss of nutrition suffered by being more highly processed means these are the least nutritious way of buying oats. High GI.

Gluten-free oats: Oats do not contain gluten but can often be contaminated with small amounts from grains on farm or milling machinery. Certified gluten-free oats have been grown, milled and packed without any contact with wheat or other gluten-containing grains.

Quick calculator

10g = 1 tablesp pinhead or medium oatmeal, or 2 tablesp rolled oats.

1 US cup = 200g pinhead or medium oatmeal, or 100g jumbo or rolled oats.

Goldilocks and the Three Bears

Breakfast

Porridge

The large area in supermarkets devoted to breakfast oats and porridge varieties – not to mention recent innovations like Stoats porridge bars – demonstrates the popularity of this wonderful breakfast food. We take it seriously in Scotland: the World Porridge Making Championships, held every 10 October (World Porridge Day*) since 1994, is hotly contested. As well as traditional porridge (oatmeal, water and salt only), there is a speciality category which can contain any other ingredient and it's great to see people experimenting.

But ever since Goldilocks scoffed Baby Bear's bowl of 'just right' porridge, there has been much debate about what makes porridge perfect. The purist may scorn porridge made from quick oats, milk and sugar, but the simple answer is that what you like to eat best is the perfect porridge.

The porridge recipes below explain how to use the different types of oats, and leave the porridge unadorned, but you can add whatever you like – the choice is endless. We love to add a good puddle of stewed blackcurrants to contrast with the cream, but you could just add sugar, evaporated milk, honey, maple or golden syrup, chopped nuts, raspberries or other berries either fresh or stewed, bananas or other fresh fruit, jam, spices such as cinnamon or cardamom, or even grated or powdered chocolate.

---

*Oatmeal Day in the USA is 9 February – perhaps an ex-pat Scots tradition going back to the February Meal Monday holiday.

Traditional Scots porridge

Ideally this is eaten from a wooden bowl with a horn spoon, and the tradition of having your cream in a separate bowl is sensible as it stays cold and the porridge hot, producing a far from Spartan meal. To produce a really nutty flavour, toast the oatmeal first.

Serves 2
600ml (1 pint) water
80g (3oz) medium oatmeal
¼ teasp salt

The accepted method is to bring the water and salt to the boil and add the oatmeal in a thin stream while stirring the water briskly with a spurtle★ or wooden spoon, to avoid lumps forming. However, you can also stir oatmeal into cold water and bring it to the boil. Simmer for 7–10 minutes then serve, with or without cream and sugar. If you like creamier porridge with a little less 'bite', cook it for up to 15 minutes.

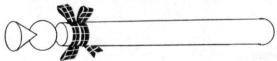

★A spurtle is just a stick, like the handle of a wooden spoon, but I find a 'spon' – a double-backed spoon invented by Neal Robertson of Auchtermuchty – works a treat. Neal won the World Porridge Championships in 2010 and 2011.

Overnight pinhead porridge

In this version, pinhead oatmeal (or for a more extreme example, oat groats) is cooked overnight in a range oven to produce a sublime, slightly popping texture. If you want to make it on the hob, soak the oats in their water overnight and then simmer them for about 20 minutes, otherwise they take a long time to cook from scratch.

Serves 2
80g (3oz) pinhead oatmeal or oat groats
600ml (1 pint) water
¼ teasp salt

Stir the oatmeal into the water and add the salt. Bring to the boil, stir, then cover the pan and place in the lowest oven and leave it overnight. Depending on how hot your oven is and how long you sleep, it may be necessary to add a little water in the morning.

Rolled oat porridge

Once oats are cut, steamed and rolled to make 'porage oats' they cook more quickly than oatmeal, but the main difference between the two is the texture – rolled oats give a smoother feel. Either water or milk (or half and half) can be used.

Serves 2
80g (3oz) rolled or jumbo oats
600ml (1 pint) milk or water
¼ teasp salt
2 teasp sugar (optional)

Put the oats into a pan and stir in the liquid. Bring to the boil and simmer for 3 minutes. Jumbo oats will take about 10 minutes.

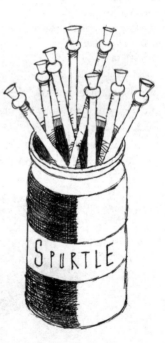

Microwave porridge

This is a fine way to make porridge for one person. It makes most sense with rolled oats, because unless medium oatmeal is soaked overnight it is quicker to cook it on the hob.

Serves 1
40g (1½ oz or 8 tablesp) rolled oats
Pinch of salt and/or 1 teasp sugar
300ml (½ pint) water or milk
Toppings to taste

Put the rolled oats into a generous-sized cereal bowl with the liquid and cook on high (900w) for 2 minutes, then stir and cook for a further 2 minutes. Leave to stand for 30 seconds before seasoning and serving with your favoured flavourings.

To make microwave porridge using oatmeal, put 40g (1½ oz) medium or pinhead oatmeal into a large cereal bowl with 300ml (½ pint) water or milk and leave it to soak overnight. Then cook on high for 2 minutes, stir, and cook for another 2 minutes.

Office porridge

The notion of the porridge drawer into which a week's
supply of porridge was cooked and tipped has been the
subject of much mirth but it is not such a silly idea.
People who are too busy to cook in the morning have
now started to use
this modern
equivalent of the
porridge-drawer
again. A week's
supply of porridge
is made in advance, by any
of the methods above. Then it
is cooled, divided into portions
which are kept in the fridge, and
heated up in the microwave,
either at home or in the office
after a bracing cycle ride.

Martha's almond muesli

The original Swiss Bircher muesli dates from 1900 and used, per person, 2 fresh whole apples (core and skin included) grated into 1 tablespoon each of: rolled oats (soaked overnight in water), whole nuts, cream, and honey plus the juice of half a lemon.

Many people now make their own version – in the summer we simply have rolled oats with raspberries and milk or cream. Here is my daughter Martha's muesli – the almonds lend richness and nutrition. Alter the proportions to taste and if the fruit is not very sweet it will need honey.

Serves 1
50g (2oz) rolled oats
15g (2 tablesp) ground almonds
100g (4oz) plain yoghurt
Handful of berries or other fruit
Honey to taste

Mix the dry ingredients together, then stir in the yoghurt and some honey if needed. Finally add the fruit. Eaten at once, this is quite soft. If you make extra and leave some till the next day, it firms up and will need extra yoghurt or milk to loosen it. Both versions are delicious, just different.

Granola and granola bars

A lot of shop-bought granola has a shocking amount of sugar, but when you make your own, you are in control. For anyone who has to take their breakfast on the run, a granola bar makes a balanced meal. Clearly you can substitute different ingredients. Sharp flavoured dried fruits like cranberries or raspberries are good.

150g (5½ oz) jumbo rolled oats
2 tablesp oat bran (optional)
3 tablesp sunflower seeds
3 tablesp pumpkin seeds
60g (2oz) chopped nuts
150g (5½ oz) dried fruit, chopped
3 tablesp almond or peanut butter
5 tablesp honey
1 teasp vanilla essence (optional)

Preheat the oven to 160°C (325°F, Gas 3). Line a shallow baking tray 20 x 30cm (8 x 12in) with baking parchment.

Mix all the dry ingredients together. Warm the nut butter, honey and vanilla together until really runny and stir this into the dry mix. Keep stirring until it is thoroughly coated with the liquid. To make granola, tip it into the tin and spread it out loosely. For granola bars, press it firmly into the tin and smooth it till flat and even.

Bake for 20–25 minutes, until the grains are beginning to colour. For granola, simply allow it to cool,

then store it in an airtight jar. For granola bars, remove
from the oven and press the mixture back down into the
tin. Allow it to cool completely before turning it out onto
a board and cutting into slices with a very sharp knife.

Butter brose

If you don't like sweet things for breakfast or don't have time to cook porridge then perhaps brose is the answer. This, as F. Marian McNeill says, 'has been the backbone of many a sturdy Scotsman.' You can also make it with hot milk instead of water. Sweet forms of brose involve adding toasted oatmeal to whipped cream, leaving it to thicken, and adding fruit and honey. Meal crowdie or butter brose is even simpler – simply pour cold water or buttermilk over your oatmeal until it is the thickness of pancake batter, and eat it with or without salt.

Serves 1
3 tablesp medium oatmeal
¼ teasp salt (less if preferred)
30g (1oz) butter
Boiling water
Buttermilk or milk to serve

Put the oatmeal into a big cereal bowl with the salt and butter, and pour over enough boiling water to generously cover it, stirring it to remove lumps. Eat at once.

Knotty Tams

Much loved in the past, Knotty Tams can best be described as a form of mini dumpling. They are lumps of undercooked oatmeal formed when oatmeal is dumped, all at once, into boiling milk or water. They were sometimes purposefully formed in porridge and soups, or served as a supper dish.

To make one portion, bring 200ml (7 fl. oz) stock, water or milk to a rolling boil, then add 40g (2oz) oatmeal and stir. Cook for about 10 minutes and serve with salt or sugar.

Caulders

Who has not, in their time, made too much porridge and, without a porridge drawer to keep it in, has guiltily peeled off the layer on the bottom of the pan and thrown it away? Here is another great warming savoury dish that should be more widely known and is particularly good with punchy flavours like kippers or bacon.

The word 'caulders'or 'calders' comes from 'cauld', as in cold porridge. The porridge should be as stiff as possible, so cook off as much water as you can before letting it cool. Unless you like sweet and savoury together, make the porridge without sugar.

Serves 1
Streaky bacon or a kipper
Cold cooked porridge
Medium oatmeal

Gently fry your bacon or kipper so that the fat or oil acquires its flavour. Remove and keep warm. Take some cold porridge and, just like making thin fishcakes, form it into little patties by coating it with oatmeal, then fry it gently in the flavoured fat until heated through and crisp and brown on the outside. Serve with the bacon or kipper, and a fried egg as well if really hungry.

Try also ... oatcakes and others

Sometimes it's hard to know in which section to place recipes. Here are some other foods that make a good breakfast.

Oatcakes – pages 75-86. Oatcakes make a wonderful breakfast, in particular the rough oatcakes spread with butter. If that's not enough, have some cheese with them and an apple. You won't feel hungry again for hours.

Orange and cardamom oatmeal custard – page 71. This is a breakfast for real hedonists. Sweet, fragrant and creamy, you almost have to eat it in bed and then snuggle down again. Mmm.

Yeasted oat pancakes – page 51. Made in advance and warmed through quickly, you can simply roll them up with butter and jam or some fresh fruit and yoghurt, or have them savoury with mushrooms and tomatoes, or bacon and scrambled egg as fillings.

Fruit pots with caramelised oats – page 68. Made with yoghurt, this makes a luxurious breakfast dish for a weekend treat.

Soups and savoury dishes

Mussel brose
(Scottish moules marinières)

Mussels are found all round the rocky coasts of Scotland
so this creamy soup is not associated with any particular
region, though perhaps Musselburgh – famed for
centuries for its mussel beds – might claim the dish as its
own. The original versions don't use wine or garlic and
have 'Knotty Tams' in them (see page 31) but mine is a
sort of Auld Alliance between the Scots version and
moules marinière.

Serves 4
Butter
1 onion, chopped
2 cloves garlic, crushed
300ml (½ pint) dry white wine
1kg (2¼ lb) mussels, washed and de-bearded
100g (4oz) onion
100g (4oz) leeks
100g (4oz) celery
2 tablesp medium oatmeal, toasted
250ml (8 fl. oz) milk
6 tablesp double cream
Parsley, fennel, chervil, chopped

Soften the onion and garlic in butter, then add the wine
and simmer for a few minutes. Add the mussels (omitting
any that won't close or are broken), put a lid on the pan,

and cook for a few minutes until the mussels have opened. Drain the mussels (discarding any that remain closed) and reserve the liquid, straining off any grit. When cool, take out the meat, and remove any bits of beard.

Dice the onion, leek and celery very small and cook them gently in butter until transparent and nearly cooked, then stir in the oatmeal. Add some of the mussel broth and stir until smooth, then stir the rest in gradually, with the milk. Simmer gently for 10–15 minutes until the oatmeal has thickened. Then season with pepper – and salt only if needed – and stir in the cream, adding milk, water or lemon juice if needed. Add the mussels and warm them through gently for a minute or two, then stir in the herbs and serve at once.

Nettle kail

Nettle soup is a good springtime tonic after a dreich winter. Just pick the top few tender nettle leaves – wear gloves to handle them. If there are no nettles, this is also good with spinach or watercress, and garlic instead of wild garlic leaves. The oatmeal thickens the soup like miniature pearl barley.

Serves 6
2 leeks, washed and chopped
4 handfuls wild garlic leaves or 2 cloves garlic, chopped
1.2 litres (2 pints) excellent poultry stock
4 tablesp medium oatmeal
200g (8oz) young nettle tops or spinach
Salt & pepper

Sweat the leek, and chopped garlic if used, gently in oil or butter, then add the oatmeal and chopped wild garlic leaves and stir for a few minutes. Add half the stock and simmer for 5 or 6 minutes, then blend until smooth. Return to the pan, add the remaining stock and simmer for 5 more minutes. Meanwhile chop the nettle leaves finely, add them to the soup and cook until they are soft but still bright green. Add salt and pepper to taste.

Skirlie

This much-loved and very traditional concoction is endlessly versatile. It can be used as a stuffing or as a side dish with chicken, or scattered over vegetables (traditionally potatoes) or anything you like. Wherever fried breadcrumbs would be good, try skirlie instead. You can also make skirlie with jumbo oats if a very rough texture is wanted.

---

1 small onion, chopped
25g (1oz) beef dripping, or bacon fat
80g (3oz) medium or pinhead oatmeal
Salt & pepper

Fry the onion slowly in the fat, then add the oatmeal and stir (or 'skirl') it around the pan until it has absorbed all the fat and the oatmeal is thoroughly cooked and toasted brown. Season well. This is often served with boiled potatoes and very good it is too.

Pheasant breasts with bacon skirlie

The Scottish version of fried breadcrumbs, skirlie goes
especially well with lean game birds, whether grouse,

*Skirlie goes especially well with
lean game birds....
We'll be OK, then.*

partridge, pigeon or, in this case, pheasant. The bacon makes it salty, though, so don't season the skirlie too much. Serve with excellent mashed potato and perhaps leeks in a bechamel sauce.

Serves 4

4 rashers streaky bacon
Skirlie (as in the preceding recipe)
4 medium pheasant breasts
300ml (½ pint) game or beef stock
20 juniper berries, crushed
2 teasp redcurrant or rowan jelly

Chop the bacon into tiny pieces and gently fry them in the minimum of fat until they are really crisp. Stir this into the skirlie and keep it warm.

Fry the pheasant breasts in the bacon pan with a little extra butter, making sure they are nicely browned. Slightly undercook them, then remove them and keep warm. Add the juniper berries to the pan and fry gently for a few minutes, then add the stock and boil it rapidly until it reduces by half. Remove the juniper berries and add the jelly, stirring until it is dissolved, then boil until syrupy. Season with salt and pepper.

Now slice the pheasant breasts. If they are too pink, add the slices to the pan of warm sauce and gently stir them around for a minute until they are no longer too pink. Never allow it to as much as simmer or the meat will toughen. Serve with the bacon skirlie and vegetables.

Ham and haddie

Some years ago we did a series of demonstrations to chefs to encourage the use of old Scottish recipes with a modern twist. Ham and haddie was one of mine. The original is fried ham slices or bacon, served with fried

Haddies

Ham

JUMBO OATS

MILK

Butter

Chives   Parsley

smoked haddock. In my new twist the crisp, bacony skirlie and delicate flaked fish make a good combination. Courgettes go really well with this.

Serves 2

2 large or 4 small unsmoked haddock fillets
Milk
1 lemon
Butter or rapeseed oil
4 rashers streaky bacon, chopped
1 small onion, chopped
4 tablesp jumbo oats
Chopped herbs (such as chives, parsley, fennel)

Preheat the oven to 180°C (350°F, Gas 4). Cut the fillets in two lengthways and roll them up, leaving the thin end on the outside. Secure with cocktail sticks. Put them in a close-fitting dish and pour a little milk over them. Season with pepper and the grated zest of the lemon. Cover with foil and bake for 10–15 minutes, until only just cooked.

Meanwhile slowly fry the bacon snippets in butter or oil until they are crisp and have rendered their fat. Remove and keep warm. Cook the onions in the remaining fat until soft. Add another tablespoon of oil, add the oats and stir. Cook over a medium heat until the oats are cooked and all the fat is absorbed. Return the bacon snippets with the herbs and serve beside (not under) the haddock.

Pork and kale and knockit corn

This is a great winter dish, the bittersweet kale counter-acting the pork and oats perfectly. I've made it for years using pearl barley but oats are fantastic too. 'Knockit corn' is a Shetland term, coming from the sound of the husk being knocked off the corn to leave the groats. Use a fatty cut of pork for this dish. If shoulder steaks don't have enough, use belly but trim off some of the excess fat. Only the soft leaves of the kale are used here – any tough stalks should be cut out.

Serves 4

700g (1½ lb) fatty pork, diced
200g (6oz) oat groats
300ml (½ pint) beef or chicken stock
120g kale, chopped and stalks removed
Salt & pepper

In a large, heavy-bottomed pan, put a tablespoon of oil and add the pork, fatty side down. Cook gently so that the fat starts to melt out, then increase the heat to brown the meat really well. It should be deep brown all over. Add the stock and the oats and bring to simmering point. Cover tightly and allow it to barely simmer for 1½ – 2 hours, giving it an occasional stir so that it doesn't stick to the bottom. If it gets too dry, add a little water. It should end up cooked but with a firm and slightly crunchy texture. Season to taste and then add the kale to the dish, stirring it in well. Cook for another 5 minutes, no more, until the kale has softened but is still dark green, lending the dish a bittersweet flavour.

Avenotto (oat risotto) with oat groats

Oat groats make a wonderful risotto, more akin to rice than barley but they take a lot longer to cook – even after soaking them they need 1–1½ hours to cook. However, this also means it can be prepared in advance without overcooking; just the peas and herbs need adding at the last minute. This version contains meat but it's also lovely with just vegetables. The quantities and varieties are not critical so change them or add others according to taste (mushrooms are good). The better the stock is, the better will be the result. It's a good use for leftover roast poultry.

Serves 3–4

150g (5½ oz) oat groats
600ml (1 pint) poultry or vegetable stock
Rapeseed or olive oil
1 onion, chopped
2 carrots, diced small
1 leek, cleaned and sliced
100g (4oz) celery, diced small
250g (9oz) cooked poultry meat
Handful of peas – frozen is fine
2 handfuls fresh herbs (such as parsley, coriander, chervil)
optional: mushrooms, lemon zest, white wine, grated cheese

If possible, soak the groats in 150ml (¼ pint) of the stock for 8 hours or overnight. Using a large frying pan, gently

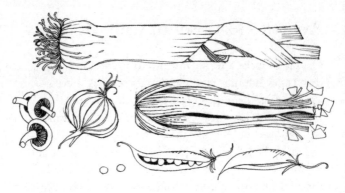

fry the onion and carrot in a good quantity of oil for 5 minutes. Then add the groats and enough stock to cover them. Simmer very gently for 45 minutes, stirring well from time to time and topping up with more stock as it starts to dry – watch it doesn't stick to the bottom. Add mushrooms now, if using, and season well with coarsely ground black pepper.

Meanwhile boil the leek and celery until barely cooked and still a nice bright green. Drain, and reserve their broth to use as stock. If all the stock gets used up, top up with water if needed. After 1¼ hours, season with salt and taste. If a more acidic flavour is wanted, add the grated zest of a lemon and/or a dash of white wine. Then add the poultry meat, the cooked leek and celery, and finally the peas and keep turning it over so that they are all thoroughly warmed through. Just before serving, stir in a handful of grated cheese, if using, and the freshly chopped herbs.

Leek and blue cheese flan

There are many wonderful Scottish blue cheeses available these days. Most tend to be fairly salty, so only season the filling with pepper. The pastry is quite delicate but has a wonderful nutty flavour and can be used for many savoury pastry dishes. It's easier to handle several small quiche tins than one large one.

Serves 4–6

Oatmeal pastry
100g (4oz) medium oatmeal
100g (4oz) plain flour
100g (4oz) butter
1 egg, beaten

Filling
150g (5½ oz) leeks, chopped and rinsed
Butter
150ml (¼ pint) milk
100g (4oz) blue cheese
1 egg
2–3 small tomatoes

Preheat the oven to 160°C (325°F, Gas 3). Grease the quiche tins. Put the oatmeal, flour and butter into a food processor and blend until it is starting to stick together. Add half of the beaten egg and blend into a dough. Roll it out thinly on a floured board and cut out rounds to line the tins, carefully pressing it into the edges so it doesn't crack. If it does, gently press it together again or even patch them with a paste made from the scraps. Bake for 25 minutes or until the cases are light brown. Turn the oven up to 180°C (350°F, Gas 4).

Meanwhile, chop the leek into small pieces and gently fry them in butter until soft. Beat the other egg with the remaining half egg and add the milk and some pepper. Crumble the cheese. When the pastry shells are cooked, divide the leeks and crumbled cheese between them, pour over the egg and milk and put a half tomato in each one. Bake for 25 minutes and serve still warm.

Yeasted oatmeal pancakes with Arbroath smokies

Oatmeal pancakes are good enough to eat on their own with butter, or with soup instead of bread, but filled like this they make a dish in themselves. If you make these ahead and chill or freeze them, put greaseproof paper or cling film between the pancakes to prevent them sticking together. Call them galettes if you want to be trendy.

Serves 6

For the pancakes
75g (3oz) fine oatmeal or blitzed rolled oats
75g (3oz) flour
1¼ teasp (½ a 7g sachet) quick yeast
1 teasp salt
175ml (6 fl. oz) hot water
175ml (6 fl. oz) milk

Filling
3 Arbroath smokies or 450g (1lb) smoked fish
2 medium onions, chopped
1½ tablesp flour
150ml whole milk
½ teasp ground mace or nutmeg
50ml cream
Chopped parsley
Handful of peas

Mix the flours, yeast and salt. Mix the hot water with the milk, and add to the flour gradually, stirring well so there are no lumps. Cover and leave in a warm place for an hour until bubbly. Then heat a 30cm (12 inch) skillet or heavy frying pan, brush with butter and pour in a scant ladleful of the batter, swirling it round quickly to coat the whole pan thinly. If the mixture is too thick to do this, add some milk to the mixture. Once the sides start to curl, turn the pancake over using a spatula – they are a bit fragile – and cook the other side. Remove and keep warm. Repeat with the rest to make 6 large pancakes.

Discard skin and bones from the Arbroath smokies. Briefly cook the smoked fish. Gently cook the onions in a little butter until cooked but not brown. Stir in the flour, then gradually add the milk, stirring to avoid lumps forming. Add the mace and cook gently for 10 minutes until thick and creamy, then add the flaked fish, cream, parsley and peas. Cook for another few minutes until the peas are just cooked. Divide the mixture between the pancakes, roll them up and serve with mashed potato.

ARBROATH SMOKIE

NEEP

ORGANIC TATTIES

HOME MADE HAGGIS

STEAMED IN A BOWL IN A POT

Haggis at home

You couldn't have a book about oatmeal without haggis. But although it has been adopted as Scotland's national dish, savoury puddings boiled in an animal's stomach are universal and date back at least to ancient Greece – one of Aristophanes' comic plays even points out its tendency to burst. In England, written recipes for such puddings date back to around 1380 with recipes specifically for haggis (variously spelt hagga, hagus, hagges, hassisse, hackin, and so on) appearing in cookery books from the 1420s onwards, proving haggis to be commonplace English fare until well into the eighteenth century. But although haggis was also a Scots dish – William Dunbar in the 15th century wrote of a 'haggies' – curiously, it is barely mentioned in Scottish cookery books until after Robert Burns' death. Be that as it may, haggis is definitely considered to be our national dish.

This recipe is adapted from a 1920s one by F. Marian McNeill that uses venison, which in my opinion is even better than lamb – after all, Burns never mentions lamb in his poem. But if you want to make this dish using lamb or mutton, reduce the suet a bit. It's do-able to make this at home because it is steamed in a bowl – like a Christmas pudding – and doesn't contain the lungs forby. Incidentally, the plural of 'haggis' is 'haggis'.

Serves 4

100g (4oz) venison shoulder, sliced
100g (4oz) venison heart, sliced
100g (4oz) venison liver, sliced
80g (3oz) pinhead oatmeal
1 teasp salt
½ teasp black pepper
¼ teasp each of ginger and nutmeg
1 onion, finely chopped
80g (3oz) venison or beef suet, grated

Cover the meats in water and simmer for 45 minutes. Toast the oatmeal in a dry frying pan, then stir in the seasonings and onion. Add a generous ladleful of the cooking broth to the oatmeal and allow it to soak while the meat cools in its broth. Drain the meats and mince or chop them finely. Add them, and the suet, to the soaked oatmeal. Add more cooking broth, if needed, to make a loose dropping mixture.

Put this into a greased 1 litre (1¾ pint) pudding basin. Cover with greased paper, tie foil tightly over the top, and put it in a pan with water coming halfway up. Cover and simmer very gently for four hours. Serve very hot from the basin onto very hot plates, with mashed potato and buttery mashed neeps. Neeps, by the way, are orange turnips if you are Scots and swedes if you are English.

Try also . . .
Caulders (page 33) with herring for a lunch dish

Desserts

Ginger and whisky cranachan

Cranachan (also known as cream crowdie) is whipped cream with crunchy oatmeal, whisky, honey and soft fresh raspberries stirred into it or, if you are unlucky, a stodgy mass of cold cream porridge with squashed frozen raspberries.

My variation is a great stomach-warmer for the winter – whisky and ginger being a perfect combination. It's powerful so the portions are quite small. The only secret to making good cranachan is that the oatmeal must be toasted, and stirred in right at the last minute, otherwise it absorbs liquid from the cream and turns both into a dull solid mass. You could even have separate bowls of the three ingredients on the table and get people to mix it themselves.

Serves 6
4 tablesp blended whisky
80g (4oz) dried crystallised ginger
80g (3oz) medium oatmeal
450ml (¾ pint) double or whipping cream

Chop the ginger pieces into small chunks. Put them in a jar with the whisky, put the lid on the jar and shake it. Leave for at least a day, shaking it from time to time, for the whisky to soak into it (longer is better and it keeps indefinitely).

Toast the oatmeal and allow it to cool completely.
Just before you need to serve it, whip the cream very
lightly – no more, as the oatmeal quickly stiffens it. Then
stir in the ginger pieces and finally the oatmeal with
some of the sweetened whisky to taste. If you do have to
keep it and it goes a bit too stiff, stir in more whisky or
milk to loosen it. Spoon into individual glasses and serve
immediately. It is filling!

Wheat-free spiced apple cake

This cake is light and slightly crumbly with the apples making a good foil to the spices. This makes two cakes so you could leave the apples out of one and simply use it as a cake. If you don't want to serve them immediately, they can be kept in a warm oven for a while, or else gently reheated from cold.

Makes two cakes
2 tablesp golden caster sugar
4 apples
175g (6oz) rolled oats or oat flour
175g (6oz) butter, cut into chunks
175g (6oz) soft brown sugar
Grated zest of 1 orange
4 eggs
3 teasp baking powder
2 teasp ground cinnamon
½ teasp ground cloves
1 teasp ground nutmeg
2 teasp ground ginger

Preheat the oven to 180°C (350°F, Gas 4). Line the base of a 20cm (8 inch) diameter cake tin, and butter it all over. Scatter the caster sugar over the bottom of the tins. Peel, core and slice the apples and lay them on the base of the tins, making a pattern with them if you wish.

If using rolled oats instead of oat flour, blitz them in

the small bowl of a food processor until it is the consistency of fine wholewheat flour.

Beat the butter and sugar together until pale and creamy, then beat in the orange zest and eggs. Mix the baking powder and all the spices into the oat flour, and add half of this into the butter/sugar mixture. Mix briefly, then add the rest and mix until smooth. Pour the mixture over the sliced apples in the tin and bake for 30–35 minutes, or until the cake begins to shrink from the side of the tin and a skewer comes out clean. Leave it for a few minutes before turning it out onto a plate.

Tip: *If you pop the lined tins into the oven for a few seconds to warm, it makes buttering them really easy.*

PRALINE

SUGAR

WATER

MEDIUM OATMEAL

ICE CREAM

SUGAR

2 EGG WHITES

LIQUEUR

VANILLA ESSENCE

WHIPPING CREAM

Oatmeal praline ice cream with hot chocolate sauce

The 'praline', made from oatmeal cooked in boiling syrup, is remarkably like almond praline. During the process the pan gets extremely hot, so use an oven glove to hold it. It keeps well in an airtight jar and is also used to make the soufflé below so it's worth making double while you are at it.

The ice cream is great as it is, but if you want to make it more adult, add 2–3 tablespoons of whisky, brandy, or rum. You could also serve it with a raspberry purée instead of the chocolate sauce. Or try adding 50g (2oz) dried raspberries or cranberries. Chocaholics might prefer to add dark chocolate chips.

Makes 1 litre (1¾ pints)

For the praline:
50g (2oz) sugar
40ml (3 tablesp) water
50g (2oz) medium oatmeal

For the ice cream:
100g (4oz) sugar
2 egg whites
300ml (½ pint) whipping cream
1 teasp vanilla essence
2–3 tablesp spirits or liqueur (optional)

For the chocolate sauce:
110g (4oz) butter
6 tablesp golden syrup
4 tablesp cocoa powder

To make the praline, put the sugar and water into a heavy-based saucepan. (Non-stick is good but not essential.) Dissolve the sugar over a gentle heat and, once dissolved, raise the temperature and bring to a brisk boil. Add the oatmeal in a steady stream and stir it in with a thick wooden spoon, making sure there are no lumps.

Keep stirring it over a high heat, making sure to quickly scrape in any part that starts to form a brown skin on the bottom and in the corners. You want it to brown but not burn. If it starts browning too quickly at any point, remove it from the heat and keep stirring, then turn down the heat and return the pan, stirring what has now become a stiff lump. Quite suddenly it will turn pale and crumbly. At this point keep stirring, smashing up the larger lumps and scraping the brown off the bottom until you have a pan of what looks like coarse, panko-like breadcrumbs, well speckled with brown. Allow these to cool.

Whip the eggs to form stiff peaks and fold in the caster sugar to make a meringue. Whip the cream to form soft peaks and fold this into the meringue. If using spirits, stir it into the praline now. Fold the praline into the meringue and turn into freezing container(s). Freeze

until solid. Place in the fridge for half an hour before serving to soften it.

To make the sauce, put the butter, syrup and cocoa powder into a small pan and gently melt them all together. Allow it to bubble slowly for a few minutes. If it gets too thick, add a splash of water. Serve in a warm jug with the ice cream.

Whisky and oatmeal praline soufflé

This is my Scottish take on an Italian almond and brandy pudding. Use a light or blended whisky, not a smoked or peaty one. Good alternatives are brandy, rum, Cointreau or Grand Marnier. It has the consistency of a spongy cake and must be eaten straight from the oven with plenty of pouring cream, but you could equally well serve either a raspberry pureé or the chocolate sauce above.

Serves 3–4
Praline from the previous recipe
2 egg whites
20ml (2–3 tablesp) whisky or other spirits

Make the praline as in the previous recipe. To make the soufflé, preheat the oven to 180°C (350°F, Gas 4). Butter individual soufflé dishes or ramekins. Beat the egg whites until stiff. Stir the whisky into the oatmeal praline and immediately fold this into the egg whites. Spoon the mixture into the dishes and bake for ½ – ¾ hour. It will not rise much.

Fruit pots with caramelised oats

This delicious and very simple dessert can be assembled in advance, except for the topping which should be added just before serving so that it doesn't soften. The amounts given are not critical; this is enough for a small wine glass but some people will happily consume a bowlful, so my quantities are just a guideline.

Oatmeal complements blackcurrants and rhubarb particularly well, though apples are also very good. Blackcurrants simply need stewing with enough sugar or honey to sweeten them. Stewed rhubarb benefits from the addition of chopped, grated or ground ginger. Apples are improved by a dusting of cinnamon. Cream, crème fraiche or a creamy sheep's yoghurt all work well.

Serves 1 (approx.)
4 tablesp stewed blackcurrants, rhubarb or apple
2–3 tablesp whipped cream, crème fraiche or sheep's yoghurt
1–2 crisp flapjacks (see page 91)

If the flapjacks are not crisp, bake them in the oven for 5–10 minutes to crisp up, then allow them to cool. Put a thick layer of stewed fruit in the base of a bowl or glass for each person. Whip the cream, or gently stir the crème fraiche or yoghurt, and then spread a generous layer on top of the fruit. Crumble the flapjacks into coarse crumbs and scatter a good layer on top just before serving.

Orange and cardamom baked oatmeal custard

If you like rice pudding, try this. As well as a dessert it makes the most hedonistic breakfast ever. The cardamom gives a lovely fragrance. I don't think it needs anything extra, but if you want added sharpness, serve with the orange peel garnish. A sharp marmalade sauce would also go well.

Serves 4–6

60g (2oz) pinhead oats or groats
300ml (½ pint) + 75ml full-cream milk
30g (1oz) caster sugar
4 cardamom pods
75ml (2½ fl. oz) single cream
75ml (2½ fl. oz) full-cream milk
1 large egg
Juice & grated zest of 1 unwaxed orange
Butter to grease dishes

Garnish (optional)
1 unwaxed orange
2 tablesp sugar
2 tablesp water

Put the oats into a saucepan with the sugar and 300ml (½ pint) of the milk and stir over a medium heat for 20–30 minutes to make a soft porridge (groats will need longer).

Crush the cardamom pods, remove the husks, and grind the seeds, adding them to the oats while they cook. Allow the mixture to cool down a bit. While it cools, preheat oven to 140°C (275°F, Gas 1).

Beat the egg in a bowl. Finely grate the zest off the orange, squeeze out the juice, and add these to the egg with the cream and remaining milk. When the oatmeal has cooled slightly, add it to the egg mixture. This will yield 600–700ml (a generous pint). Stir thoroughly and turn it into ramekins or a shallow dish and bake it in the oven. Ramekins will be cooked in 35 minutes and a larger dish needs 40–45 minutes depending on depth. Serve warm.

To make the garnish, pare the peel off the orange and cut it into very thin julienne strips. In a small pan, dissolve the sugar in the water and bring to a simmer. Add the orange zest strips and cook gently until they become transparent. Then leave them to cool and drain first before strewing them over the custards.

Try also . . .
Yeasted oatmeal pancakes (page 51). Fill them with stewed apple or rhubarb spiced with some grated ginger, and serve the pancakes with crème fraîche or cream cheese.

Baking

MEDIUM
Oatmeal

THE
PERFECT
OATCAKE

TOASTING

Making the perfect oatcake

The perfect oatcake is infinitely variable and ultimately a matter of personal choice. Thick and crumbly? Fine and crisp? Dark? Pale? Sweet? Cheesy? Coarse? Smooth? Texture and flavour are determined by the proportions and types of ingredients. Homemade oatcakes are not only far better than shop-bought ones (because you've perfected them to your individual preference), but they are also enormously cheaper and well worth making if you eat a lot.

Oatmeal. Starting with the oats, medium oatmeal is used in all recipes. But to make a coarser texture, either pinhead oatmeal and/or rolled oats are added, and some people like to include seeds (pumpkin, linseed, sunflower for example), or chopped nuts. To make thinner oatcakes, some fine oatmeal or oat flour is used instead.

Toasting oatmeal and rolled oats. This brings out the nutty flavour, and refreshes oats that may have been in the packet too long. It also crisps up rolled oats, which can otherwise be a bit flabby. Small quantities can be done in a dry frying pan over a medium heat. You need to keep turning it so they don't burn on the bottom. Stop when most are slightly coloured. For larger quantities the oven is easier, though make sure you check them regularly as they can burn quickly.

Flour. Adding wheat flour makes oatcakes less fragile, so it is good for making thin, crisp oatcakes, but using too much flour makes them hard. When I have it, I love to use beremeal instead of wheat flour as it gives a slightly smoky flavour.

Water. The less water you use, the more crumbly the oatcakes will be. Therefore oatcakes made from the offcuts that need more water to bind them tend to be a little harder; this is more the case when using wheat flour. Most recipes use hot water because this helps to bind the oats together.

Fat. The more fat (especially soft fats like lard, oil and chicken fat) there is, the 'shorter' and more fragile the oatcakes will be. Beef dripping gives a wonderful rich flavour. Butter makes them crisper than lard, as well as making them taste dangerously more-ish; I usually go for half butter and half lard or dripping.

Shape. In the past, when they were cooked on round girdles over the fire, the most efficient shape was a large round (correctly called a bannock) which was cut into quarters (farls) before going onto the girdle. Small rounds are oatcakes, and of course there is no reason why they should not be cut into squares, which would make the most efficient use of a modern rectangular baking tray.

FLOUR

WATER

FAT

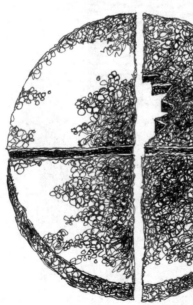

FARLS

Cooking. When oatcakes cook, the largest part of the process is spent in driving off the water. Once that has happened, the temperature rises quickly and the oatmeal starts to cook in earnest. No matter what temperature guides are given, all ovens cook slightly differently, so it's best to watch oatcakes keenly and check them regularly, especially for the last 10 minutes or so, as they can burn very quickly. The trays may need turning in some ovens (especially range ovens) whereas fan ovens will cook more evenly, but quickly. Fan ovens run at about 10°C (20°F) hotter than non-fan ovens.

Storing. Like most oatmeal products, oatcakes are at their best when really fresh. Traditionally, they were stored buried in the meal girnel (an oatmeal chest) but they will keep fine in an airtight tin. You could keep them buried in oatmeal in the tin though I must say mine never last long enough for that to be a problem and it seems a bit of a waste of good oatmeal to me. If they do lose their crisp freshness, they can be revived in a warm oven for 10–15 minutes and allowed to cool. If I make large quantities in advance, I store them in the freezer which works much better than a tin.

MEAL GIRNEL

Traditional girdle oatcakes

Because oatcake dough stiffens quickly, it is easiest to make these in batches so that as one round is cooking, the next is being rolled out. Originally, oatcakes were cooked over an open fire on a heavy iron girdle and then finished by drying them on a stone in front of the fire. A heavy frying pan over a medium heat on the hob is the nearest modern equivalent, but you can also cook these on non-stick baking sheets on a range cooker, using the hot plate to start them off and the cooler plate or oven to finish and dry them.

Makes 4–8 farls (oatcake segments)
100g (4oz) medium oatmeal
Pinch of baking powder
Pinch of salt
1 tablesp melted fat (dripping, bacon fat, butter or poultry fat)
2–3 tablesp boiling water

Put your girdle or frying pan over the fire or flame to start heating it up – don't start to mix the oatmeal until it is hot. To test, put your hand about 3cm (1 inch) over the girdle and if it feels hot but not so hot that you can't leave your hand there, it is ready. Sprinkle your board with oatmeal ready for rolling out the oatcakes.

Mix the oatmeal, baking powder and salt together and make a well in the centre. Using the handle of a wooden spoon, or a porridge spurtle, add the melted fat with just enough hot water to form a dough. Make the dough into a ball and put it on the dusted board. Quickly knead and press it out into a circle with your hands, pinching together any cracks that form, and keep dusting both sides with oatmeal to keep the surface dry. Then roll it out to about 5mm (¼ inch) thick. The best oatcakes are made with a notched rolling pin that leaves ridges on the surface, which allows air to circulate during the cooking. If you want a neat circle, put a plate over the dough and cut round it. Then cut it into four or more segments (farls).

Put these triangles onto the girdle, notched side down, and bake them until the edges start curling up. Then remove from the girdle and dry them off completely. If you're not using the original toasting stone method, dry them in a cool oven (140°C, 275°F, Gas 1) for about 25 minutes. They should snap easily when quite dry. To cook them in the oven, place the oatcakes on a greased baking sheet and bake for 20–25 minutes at 170°C (325°F, Gas 3) until firm and crisp.

Auchtermuchty oatcakes

As all the many words that have been written about
oatcakes suggest, the secret to success is to make sure they
dry out, cook evenly, and don't fall to pieces. My small
contribution to the oatmeal story is simply to bake them
on wire cooling racks, which makes sure they both cook
and dry evenly without soggy centres or burnt rims. As
they are a bit fragile, I use a small (6cm / 2½ inch
diameter) cutter or you can cut the dough into squares.

Makes about 30

225g (8oz) medium oatmeal (or ¾ medium and ¼ pinhead)
110g (4oz) plain flour, oat flour or beremeal
1 teasp baking powder
1–1½ teasp salt
80g (3oz) fat (see notes above)
75–100ml (3–3½ fl. oz) water

Heat the oven to 190°C (375°F, Gas 5). Mix the oatmeal,
flour, baking powder and salt together, then rub in the
fat. Now add just enough water to allow the ingredients
to stick together to form a dough.

Cover a board with oatmeal or flour. First press and
then roll out the dough as quickly as possible (before it
stiffens), until it is about 3mm (⅛ inch) thick. Dust the
surface of the dough to prevent it sticking and, as it will
probably crack as you roll it out, roll it in different direc-

82

tions and pinch the dough together to close the cracks, or cut round them. Cut out the oatcakes and place them close together on the racks. Crumble the offcuts and sprinkle a little water over them to form more dough, and roll out to make more oatcakes.

Bake in the oven for 25 minutes, then check and turn the racks if necessary. Now check every five minutes, because once dry, they will cook very quickly so can easily burn. They are done when they are evenly pale to golden brown. If unsure, try to break one (but remember how hot they are). If it snaps easily, it is cooked. If it bends first, cook for a little longer.

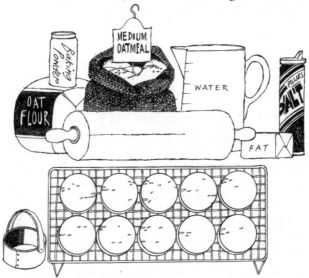

Chunky pinhead oatcakes

These are thick and crunchy and excellent with cheese, or just to nibble on their own or with butter. Those who like a slightly sweet biscuit may like to add a teaspoon of sugar. You can also add seeds or chopped nuts to make them even more highly textured. If you find these too crumbly, add 30–50g (1–2oz) plain flour next time.

Makes about 12 large oatcakes
60g (2oz) rolled oats (include pumpkin seeds, linseed,
    or nuts if you wish)
175g (6oz) medium oatmeal
60g (2oz) pinhead oats
½ –1 teasp salt
75g (2½ oz) butter, other fat or oil
5 tablesp water

Preheat the oven to 190°C (375°F, Gas 5). Stir the rolled oats (and nuts, seeds etc) in a pan over a medium high heat until you smell their gorgeous nutty aroma. Then tip them onto your board ready for forming the oatcakes.

In a small pan, melt the butter and salt (and sugar if used) in the water. When bubbling, stir in the medium and pinhead oatmeal. When it has formed a soft sticky dough, remove from the heat and divide it into 12 pieces. Take a 7cm (2½ inch) pastry cutter and place it on the board on top of the rolled oats. Then squash a piece of dough into the cutter and press it down with the back of

a spoon. They should be about 5mm / ¼ inch thick.
Scatter more oats on top and press them in. Slide a fish
slice underneath and lift the oatcakes onto a lightly oiled
baking tray then press them down firmly. Repeat with
the rest. Bake for 25 minutes, turning them after 20
minutes to make sure both sides are well dried out. Test
the centres, and if they still seem soft, leave them in the
oven but turn it off and leave the door ajar until they are
cool and crisp.

Cheese oatcakes

A few of these and an apple will keep you happy for
hours. You can use either of the previous two recipes to
make these, though I favour the thick ones. Add 90g
(3oz) grated cheese. Make sure the cheese is finely grated,
as coarsely grated cheese forms cheese 'blisters'. Since
most cheese is fairly salty you can reduce or leave out the
salt. You will get a quarter again more oatcakes on
account of the added cheese.

Keep an eye on them as they cook because
cheese can make them burn even more suddenly.
The 'bending' test for done-ness as decribed
above doesn't work with these because
cheese is bendy when hot. They crisp
up as they cool.

Fife bannock

Bannocks were originally cooked on a girdle over the fire but, like oatcakes, a heavy-duty frying pan works fine over the hob. Cooking this way is what gives that distinctive mottled brown surface and smoky taste. The alternative is to bake them in a hot oven where they rise more and are much more like scones. Serve bannocks immediately, with butter and jam. If you don't have buttermilk, use milk and add a teaspoon of lemon juice. Leave it for 20 minutes to thicken.

110g (4oz) medium oatmeal
180g (6oz) plain flour
4 teasp baking powder
½ teasp salt
25g (1oz) lard or butter
150–200ml (¼– ⅓ pt) buttermilk

Preheat the oven to 220°C (435°F, Gas 7) or start to heat a heavy frying pan until, when you hold your hand about 3cm (1 inch) over the pan, it feels hot but not uncomfortably so (see p.80). Meanwhile, mix the dry ingredients together and rub in the fat. Stir in enough buttermilk to make a soft dough and turn it out onto a well-floured board. Form it into a circle about 2.5cm (1 inch) thick for baking and about 1cm (½ in) for girdle cooking, then cut it into six wedges. For baking, gently transfer the wedges to a floured baking sheet and cook for 20 minutes. For girdle cooking, place the wedges onto the hot frying pan for 4 minutes, then turn them over for another 4 minutes. Then keep turning them so both sides are nicely browned and the bannock is cooked through.

Sauty bannocks
(oatmeal drop scones)

Drop scones are just the best thing to make when people turn up unexpectedly as they are so quick to make and so good to eat. You can make lots of these and freeze them too. Bite-sized ones make great canapés with cream cheese and smoked salmon or venison – much nicer than oatcakes.

There seems to be some difference of opinion about what 'sauty' in the title means. Some think it means 'salty' because salty oatmeal bannocks were made to induce dreams at Hallowe'en. Another version is that it comes from 'sooty' because of a tradition in the north-east of adding a little soot for luck at Hallowe'en and Shrove Tuesday. Others say it comes from the French 'sauté' meaning 'tossed' because they are flipped over. Take your pick, and add extra soot or salt if you want luck or dreams.

Makes 20–30
120g (4oz) oat flour or blitzed rolled oats
½ teasp baking soda
½ teasp salt
2 large eggs, beaten
2 teasp honey
300ml (½ pint) milk (approx.)

Mix the dry ingredients together in a bowl or jug. Make a well in the centre and add the eggs and honey. Add in the oatmeal and as soon as it becomes too stiff, add a splash of milk. Keep on adding the milk until it is thick and creamy.

Heat a large, heavy frying pan (or girdle if you have one) until, when you hold your hand about 3cm (1 inch) over the pan, it feels hot but not uncomfortably so. You can also use the simmering plate of an Aga with a baking sheet placed on top. Smear it with a thin film of butter. Use a ladle to drop circles of batter about 75mm (3 inch) wide onto the hot surface. Let them cook until there is only a small circle of uncooked batter in the centre, then flip them over with a spatula – they should be nicely browned. Cook the other side then remove, and cover them with a cloth to prevent them drying up. Cook the rest in the same way and serve them warm.

Flapjacks

Flapjacks were originally small pancakes, the word 'flap'
meaning 'to flip' and 'jack' meaning small. In America,
flapjacks are still what we call pancakes, so be warned.
These buttery rolled-oat slices seem to be a 20th-century
British phenomenon. This is how my mother made them
except that she used margarine, it being the 1950s. The
perfect flapjack has a crisp outside with a slightly chewy
inside, so keep an eye on them because if overdone they
become too hard. The secret is not to use too hot an
oven, or the outside starts burning before the centre is
cooked.

Makes about 24
110g (4oz) butter
2½ tablesp golden syrup
40g (1½ oz) sugar
225g (8oz) rolled oats
½ teasp bicarbonate of soda

Heat the oven to 180°C (350°F, Gas 4), and lightly oil a
shallow baking tray 20 x 30cm (8 x 12in).

Put the butter, syrup, and sugar into a pan and gently
heat until the sugar has dissolved. Then add the oats and
bicarbonate of soda and stir together until the oats are
evenly mixed with the liquid. Pack the mixture into the
baking tray and smooth the top. It should be about 1½
cm (½ inch) thick. If they are thicker than this they will

take longer to cook; if thinner they will cook more quickly.

Bake for 15 minutes and then check. The tin may need turning if one side is cooking faster than the other. Bake for another 5 minutes or so. They should be a deep, speckled golden brown with the edges just beginning to look darker.

Remove from the oven and allow the tray to cool for a minute or two, then cut the flapjack into squares with a sharp knife and slightly separate the slices. Allow them to cool in the tin for a further 15 minutes before turning them out onto a cooling rack.

Oatmeal shortcake

Toasting the oatflakes is not essential here but it gives an interesting smoky flavour to these biscuits. In the size of tin I give here – a shallow 20 x 30cm (8 x 12 in) tin – they will be 2cm thick (about 1 inch) and be slightly chewy in the middle, which is delicious. But if you prefer a crisp shortbread biscuit, divide them between two tins, which makes them half that thickness.

Makes 16–32

225g (8oz) rolled oats
100g (3½ oz) plain flour
½ teasp salt
150g (5oz) caster sugar
50g (2oz) medium oatmeal
225g (8oz) butter, chilled and chopped
Extra caster sugar to dredge

Preheat the oven to 160°C (325°F, Gas 3). Toast the rolled oats in a large frying pan until they smell lovely and nutty and are crisp and beginning to brown. Then spread them out to cool completely. Put the flour, salt and sugar into a food processor and add the cooled oats. Blend until finely ground, then add the medium oatmeal and butter and, using the pulse button, process until the butter is all incorporated. Tip the mixture into the tin(s) and press it down really flat – I use a fish slice for this. Bake for 40–50 minutes (30–35 if thinner). They should be light brown when done, no darker.

When cooked, remove from the oven and dust with some caster sugar. Cut the shortcake into squares or triangles immediately, then leave them in the tin to firm up for about 10 minutes before gently turning them out onto a wire rack to cool.

Citrus oatmeal shortbread

This was my daughter Martha's suggestion for anyone who finds shortbread a bit too sweet as there is a hint of lemon to counter it. Use the recipe above, but don't toast the oats. Then add in the grated rind of 2 lemons (or oranges if you prefer) to the mixture. These are nicest made as the thinner size.

Orkney broonie
(oatmeal gingerbread)

The use of oatmeal in this teacake makes it so similar to
Yorkshire parkin that it made me wonder whether the
recipe travelled from north to south, or vice versa, or
whether it was parallel thinking. The texture improves –
it becomes less crumbly and more sticky – if it is left in a
tin for a day or two to mature. If buttermilk is hard to
find, use fresh milk acidulated with a teaspoon of lemon
juice and leave it for 20 minutes to thicken.

175g (6oz) medium oatmeal
175g (6oz) self-raising flour
80g (3oz) butter
120g (4oz) soft brown sugar
1 heaped tablesp ground ginger
2 tablesp black treacle
Approx 150ml (¼ pint) buttermilk or soured milk
1 beaten egg

Heat the oven to 160°C (325°F, Gas 3). Butter a 450g/1lb
loaf tin and line the base.

Mix the flour and oats together in a bowl, rub in the
butter, and then mix in the sugar and ginger. In a little
pan, dissolve the treacle in the buttermilk. Stir this into
the flour mixture with the beaten egg and mix
thoroughly to make a soft dropping consistency – a

spoonful should plop off into the bowl. Scrape this into
the tin and cook for 1–1½ hours or until a skewer comes
out clean. Leave it covered for at least one day before
eating. Serve in slices spread with a good thick layer of
softened butter.

Wheat-free chocolate and beetroot cake

This cake has a wonderfully moist, velvety texture, and the best possible filling for it is whipped cream and either blackcurrant or damson jam; both are nice and tart. It doesn't rise hugely. Because it is so soft, it is especially indulgent to split each cake in two so that you have four cream-filled layers. But it is quite rich, so having two slim cakes with two layers each is perfectly alright.

180g (6oz) butter
180g (6oz) sugar
3 eggs
180g cooked grated beetroot
80g (3oz) cocoa powder
180g (6oz) oat flour or rolled oats
4 teasp baking powder

Filling
180–250g (6–9oz) blackcurrant or damson jam
200–300ml (7–10 fl. oz) whipping cream
Cocoa powder to dust

Preheat the oven to 190°C (375°F, Gas 5). If using rolled oats, blitz them to a fine flour and reserve. Cream together the butter and sugar and beat in the eggs one by one. Then beat in the grated beetroot. Mix together the oat flour and baking powder, and fold this into the mixture.

Grease and line two 20cm (8in) cake tins and divide the cake mixture beteen them, smoothing the top well for it will not change much in the oven. Bake for 25 minutes or until the sides begin to come away from the edges and a skewer comes out clean. Allow to cool for a few minutes before turning the cakes out onto a cooling rack. When cool, carefully halve the cakes (they are a bit fragile). Warm the jam and spread it on three of the layers. Whip the cream to soft peaks and spread it over the jam. Place the layers on top of each other and dust the top with cocoa powder through a small sieve.

Try also . . .
Wheat-free spiced cake (page 60). If you make the spiced apple cake without the apples on the base, this makes a lovely cake. You can eat it just as it is, or use a butter cream icing to make it into a sandwich cake.

Granola bars (page 28). Clearly these can be endlessly adapted to personal taste. Don't like raisins? Try dried cranberries or raspberries. Love chocolate chips? Throw some in. Even better, spread the top with melted chocolate, and allow to cool before cutting it into bars.

Drinks and bathing

Oatmeal smoothies

Oats are good for making smoothies because they produce a thick and creamy drink without using dairy products or banana (the most common thickeners). Apart from berries, fruits that go especially well in oat smoothies are kiwis, passion fruits and mangoes. Children love a drop or two of vanilla essence. All these recipes make one generous serving, or two smaller glasses – drink them as soon as they are made. If you want a chilled one in summertime, use frozen fruit.

Ginger, kiwi and lime oat smoothie

A real power booster for when you need a fillip.

---

1 lime (or ½ a lemon), zest & juice
2½ tablesp fine oatmeal (or blitzed rolled oats)
½–1 teasp grated fresh ginger
2–3 teasp honey
3 ripe kiwi fruit, peeled & chopped

Make the lime juice up to 60ml (2 fl. oz) with water. Put into a blender with the zest and oatmeal and blend at full power. Add ½ teasp grated ginger and 2 teasp of the honey and blend again. Finally add the kiwi fruit and blend until smooth. Taste, and add extra honey and ginger if wished.

Oatmeal and berry smoothie

2½ tablesp fine oatmeal (or blitzed rolled oats)
Juice of half an orange
2–3 teasp honey
150g mix of raspberries, blueberries or blackberries
2 tablesp plain yoghurt (optional)

Blend the oats with the orange juice and 2 teasp honey.
Add the berries and blend again. When smooth, blend in
the yoghurt (if using), with a little more honey if needed.

Kiwi, passion fruit and mango oat smoothie

½ large, ripe mango
2½ tablesp fine oatmeal (or blitzed rolled oats)
1 ripe kiwi fruit, peeled & chopped
1 passion fruit, pulp and juice
2 teasp honey
Juice of 1 large lime or ½ a lemon

Remove the stone and skin from the mango, chop the flesh, then blend to a pulp. Sprinkle in the oatmeal and blend again, then add the kiwi fruit, passion fruit, honey and lime juice. Blend, then taste and add more honey or juice if wished.

Oat milk

Alternative milks made from nuts or grains have become common in supermarkets, such is their popularity with people who are lactose intolerant. But various forms of oat milk – thin, thick or fermented – formed an important part of the traditional Scottish diet, being used for breakfast, refreshing summer thirst-quenchers or soothing bedtime drinks.

The more powerful your blender, the smoother and thicker your oat milk will be. The exact proportions are not crucial since you can make it thicker or thinner by squeezing more or less out of the mixture, using strong cheesecloth or a nut milk bag. Or, if you want a really thick textured liquid, just use it straight from the blender. The residue can be used for cooking or as a face mask (see p. 111).

Oat milk keeps for a few days in the fridge but it separates so needs shaking before use. When cooked, it thickens. It can be left plain and used as a milk substitute or else flavoured with things like fruit purées, honey, cinnamon, and chocolate.

100g (4oz) rolled oats or oat flour
750ml (1¼ pints) water
Large square of cheesecloth

If you want the milk unstrained, blitz the rolled oats first unless your blender is really powerful. Place oats and water in the blender, leave for half an hour and then blitz until it is smooth and creamy. It can be used like this – it has the consistency of drinking yoghurt. To make milk, open out the cheesecloth into a sieve or colander placed over a bowl, and pour the oat cream into it. Bring up the corners and twist them together, making quite sure the liquid can't escape. Continue twisting and squeezing the milk out of the cloth until the remaining pulp is fairly dry and crumbly; the last bit squeezed out is the most creamy. Cover the oat milk and keep it in the fridge.

Meg Dods' white caudle

Caudles, like possets, are historic treats ripe for a revival. They were usually thickened with eggs but oatmeal does the job here. Caudles are warming and comforting, but this one is also invigorating due to the wine, lemon and ginger. The quantities given are a starting-off point: you can make it sharper or sweeter to taste, or swap the wine for half quantities of whisky or brandy. Serve it hot. It makes a fine end to a dinner party and settles the stomach. It does, however, look a little odd, so serve it in tiny coffee cups, with a teaspoon to sup it and a little garnish.

Serves 4–6
250ml (8 fl. oz) homemade oat milk
1 heaped tablesp heather honey
Juice of ½ a lemon
2 tablesp dry white wine
Small pinch nutmeg
Ground ginger to serve
Lemon zest and/or a fresh herb for garnish

Pare the zest off the lemon and reserve for garnish. Put the honey and oat milk into a pan and stir while it comes slowly to the boil. It will thicken and turn slightly translucent. Add the lemon juice, wine and nutmeg. Stir all together and adjust to taste. Pour into warmed espresso coffee cups, sprinkle with ginger and garnish with some lemon peel. Serve hot.

Atholl brose

There are several versions of this famous drink,
supposedly responsible for rendering the enemies of a
15th-century Duke of Atholl incapable of fighting
because he filled their well with the mixture. Aye, right!
Some mix together whipped cream, toasted oats, honey
and whisky like a runny form of cranachan. This one,
supposedly the original, uses really thick oat milk. I like it
best just as it is – a pale coffee-coloured liqueur which is
quite more-ish – but some like to add whipped cream
before serving. If you do, only use 2 tablespoons of
honey.

2–3 tablesp honey
300ml (½ pint) whisky
100g (4oz) medium oatmeal or rolled oats
300ml (½ pint) water
1–2 tablesp whipped cream (optional)

Add the honey to the whisky and whisk it to start
dissolving. Put the oatmeal and water into a blender and
leave it to soak for ½–1 hour, then blitz for about a
minute. Then squeeze out as much thick liquid from the
oats as possible, either by pressing it hard through a metal
sieve or by wringing it through a strong muslin cloth.

This should yield about 250ml (8 fl. oz) of creamy
oat milk. Add this to the honey and whisky. Put it in a

bottle or jar and shake it all well together until dissolved. The oat milk separates out quite quickly so it needs to be shaken before serving – it keeps well. Some lightly whipped cream may be whisked in just before serving if wished, but you then need to drink the whole lot.

Blenshaw

Blenshaw is a splendid comforting drink for a cold, wet day or bedtime, not unlike Horlicks. You can flavour it with anything you like but it's most refreshing when not too sweet. Put a tablespoon of fine oatmeal into a small mug with 1 teaspoon of honey. Stir in a tablespoon of full-cream milk to make a thick paste, then add a further 4 tablespoons and top up the mug with boiling water. Grate a little nutmeg or lemon zest over the top and drink it hot.

Oatmeal for your skin

Oatmeal baths are well known to soothe itchy skin and, being mild, even help with babies' nappy rash. They can also be used for pets. But even normal skin benefits from a regular oat bath to keep it soft.

Full-strength version: Stir 50g (2oz) fine oat flour or 300 ml (½ pint) home-made oat milk into the bath. Stay in the bath for at least 15 minutes and remember that the oatmeal makes everything slippery.

Everyday version: Put a handful of rolled oats into a pop-sock or square of muslin, with lavender or other herbs if wished. Tie the bag tightly but leave the oats quite loose as they swell. Tie the bag over the tap so the hot water runs through it, and once the bath is run, allow the oats to steep in the bath for 5 minutes before squeezing the oat 'milk' out of the bag into the bath water. Soak at least 10 minutes.

Facial scrubs: Many commercial exfoliants use particles of plastic that are harmful to the environment. But oatmeal paste makes an excellent face scrub especially good for oily skin. Just mix oatmeal and water and leave it for 5 minutes to soften slightly. Rub it onto your face and rinse off after 10 minutes. Honey or scented oils can be added if wished.

Where to buy oatmeal

Rolled porridge oats are universally available in the UK but some of the other grades are less easy to find, especially outside Scotland. Health food shops are a good place to start, but if you have difficulty buying locally, here are some online stockists selling some of the less easy-to-find kinds. Some come direct from the mill.

Online and mail order stockists

Green City Wholefoods http://www.greencity.coop

Hamlyns Scottish Oatmeal http://hamlynsoats.co.uk

Oatmeal of Alford, http://www.oatmealofalford.com

Real Foods http://www.realfoods.co.uk

Stoats Oats http://www.eatstoats.com